Co

Alexander Kennedy

Amazon.com/author/alexanderkennedy

Contents

Prologue

Columbus's first oceanic crossing was the most fateful voyage in human history. People had come from Eurasia to the Americas before, of course. The Americas were first populated as early as 40,000 years before Columbus, by wanderers who ventured across the ice of the Bering Strait and then swept down to cover two continents. Polynesians may have been the next to venture from the "Old" to the "New" worlds, landing on South America's western shore. Much stronger evidence suggests that Vikings led by Leif Erikson crossed the Atlantic as far as Newfoundland around 1000 A.D. Abu Bakr II, a ruler of West African's massive, technologically advanced Malian Empire, resigned his throne in the 14th century to explore the oceans—and just might have managed to find his way to the Americas. Basque fishermen and whalers are believed by many scholars to have located the astonishing fisheries of Cape Cod a century before

Columbus, but kept the new landmass secret for commercial reasons.

But Columbus's name put them all in the shade, and rightly so, because it was only with his famous 1492 voyage that America was added to maps, and real exchange between the two continents began. The Columbian Exchange was an era of great trade and great tragedy, devastating whole civilizations, but also beginning the process to bring the world together in a global community. The transfer of plants and animals that began in 1492 fed entire nations and drove others to the brink of extinction, reshaping the face of the planet.

Yet even Columbus, for all his ambition, could not have foreseen in 1492 that he was destined to shape the rest of his millennium. That year, he was struggling just to get anyone to believe him.

It is easy to see how little faith the Spanish Crown had in his chances by the size of his fleet. Ferdinand and Isabella had agreed to bankroll him, true, but only so far as to give him three small ships and less than a hundred men. One was named the *Santa Maria*, another the *Santa Clara*, and the name of third has been lost to history; as was customary, however, the sailors gave their ships nicknames, in this case, *La Gallega*, *Niña*, and *Pinta* respectively. It is a curious historical anomaly that we remember only one of these ships today by its proper name.

Perhaps the monarchs were right to have been a bit skeptical of this Genoese adventurer. By all rights, Columbus's plan shouldn't have worked. He had correctly guessed that a ship might circumnavigate the globe, but he had drastically miscalculated the globe's size, estimating it at 15,000 rather than 25,000 miles. Had an enormous, unmissable landmass not awaited Columbus halfway around the world, he and his crew would surely have perished in the expanse of the Pacific.

But Columbus would not have seen this as luck. He believed that he was God's instrument, and he would have seen this salvation as Providence's gift to a man who had dared everything.

He and his crew confessed their sins and received absolution on August 2 in Palos, Spain, and sailed from the harbor the following day at 8 AM. The harbor would have been unusually packed that day, and ships were in high demand, for August 2 had also been the Spanish Crown's final deadline for Jews to flee from Spain or face execution.

Columbus's armada, if it could be properly called that, faced troubles from the start. The rudder of the *Pinta* broke after only three days at sea—perhaps an act of deliberate sabotage, since the ship had been pressed into service by the Crown against the will of its owners. As the fleet stopped into the Canary Islands for repairs and resupply, they heard rumors of Portuguese warships in the vicinity, seeking to capture the Spanish explorers. It's not clear whether their presence was ever anything more than talk, but whatever the case, Columbus managed to set out again without encountering them. On September 6, 1492, the three ships left the last comforts of the known world behind and set out to cross an ocean. Most of those who watched them go believed that the ships would never be seen again.

It wasn't because they believed Columbus would fall off of the edge of the world, as popular myth has it; they simply and reasonably believed that setting off onto an unknown, endless ocean was a fool's errand, probably a fatal one.

But then Columbus showed his real genius for exploration. Previous attempts to cross the Atlantic directly from the Iberian Peninsula had been rebuffed by the frightful weather of that ocean's northern portion, but by crossing at the latitude of the Canaries (28° N), Columbus took advantage of what would later be called the trade winds, dramatically boosting his speed. He would follow this latitude west until he hit China or died trying. And it's this determination that set Columbus apart from those who came before him, even from his rival explorers—this willingness to cast off into the open sea, with nothing but his compass, the stars, and Providence for guides.

Still, Columbus was practical enough to know that his crew would not share his will. Though they were making phenomenal time—despite the laggardly pace of his flagship *Santa Maria*, a vessel Columbus came to regret bringing with him—Columbus carefully maintained two sets of logs, just as an embezzler might keep two sets of books. One measured the armada's actual progress (which Columbus somewhat overestimated, hampered by the primitive navigational equipment of his day), while the second, for public consumption, showed much less progress, placing the ship reassuringly closer to known land. In late September, an island was spied beneath the setting sun that in the morning turned out to have been a mirage created by a low cloudbank. The crew wanted to continue searching for the island, but Columbus forced them to continue due west.

A few weeks into the voyage, they passed through an eerie expanse of seaweed, now known as the Sargasso Sea. They approached it with apprehension, but the ships sliced through it without difficulty. "Saw plenty weed," Columbus noted.

At around this time, he also noticed that the compass needle began to point slightly away from true north. We now understand this to be magnetic declination, by which compass needles point to magnetic north rather than true north, but no Europeans had then traveled far enough for the phenomenon to be widely known there. (It was known in China, however, so Columbus could not be said to be its discoverer.)

Columbus hid this deviation for a time, but when his officers finally noticed, there was a panic and a near-mutiny. Perhaps they really were nearing the edge of the normal world. But again Columbus insisted "he had come to go to the Indies, and so had to continue until he found them, with the help of Our Lord," and again the crew backed down in the face of his iron will. Still, they had not seen land for twenty-eight days and counting, and their courage was reaching the breaking point.

Then, on October 7, Columbus received what he believed to be his long-awaited sign from Providence. A massive flock of birds covered the sky, part of a fall migration of American golden plovers. He was sure land must be near now, and he was right—but still the men grumbled.

As Columbus's most distinguished biographer, Samuel Eliot Morison, has observed, it's unfair to portray the running conflict between Columbus and his crew as between courage and cowardice, or knowledge and superstition; in fact, had Columbus been better at math or cartography, he would have realized that his expedition was far more dangerous and uncertain than he had admitted. Rather, as Morison wrote, it was "the inevitable conflict between a man of one great, compelling idea and those who did not share it in anything like the same degree."

So with the Bahamas now only 200 miles dead ahead—unbeknownst to them, of course—the men mutinied on October 10. They would go no further into unknown waters, they declared. Columbus must turn back. Their commander pleaded with them, knowing that he could no longer fall back on authority alone. Give him three days, he asked. If they had not sighted land by then, he would agree to turn back.

As it turned out, he only needed two. The day after the would-be mutiny, a branch with a red flower floated by the *Niña*. The amount of flotsam only increased: they soon saw not only plant debris, but manmade objects go floating past. Ferdinand and Isabella had promised ten thousand maravedis, a small fortune, to the first sailor to spot land, and the rails of the ships were crowded with sailors eager for the bounty. The lucky man was Rodrigo da Triana, peering into the early morning darkness from the *Pinta*'s forecastle. Columbus later robbed him of his prize by claiming that he had spied the flickering light of a candle on the island four hours before, though it seems extremely implausible that he could have made out one of the indigenous people's fires at a distance of almost forty miles.

But in another way, it was Columbus who truly deserved it. It had been his dream to test the edge of the known map, and his navigational acumen that found the route to make it possible. And it was his discoveries that so enriched his patrons as to upend the economy of medieval Europe for good. Columbus and his men went ashore on the morning of October 12, where they were met by the astonished Taino people living on the island. Columbus knelt on the beach and prayed.

The Old World had met the New, and nothing would ever be the same.

Introduction

"Life has more imagination than we carry in our dreams..."
—**Christopher Columbus**

Around 1000 A.D., the Vikings reached land far to the west of Europe. It has been reported that explorer Leif Erikson may have established a Norse village on what was later named Newfoundland some 500 years later. It has also been suggested that Polynesian explorers may have "discovered" the Americas from the opposite coast long before even the Vikings reached their destination. Native Americans had inhabited the land for thousands of years before the Polynesians reached the land that lie between two vast oceans, but it was Christopher Columbus who won acclaim, found wealth, and made Spain an economic power when he set sail searching for a westward trade route between Europe and Asia.

While his intent was to establish a sea route to eliminate the need to sail east around the continent of Africa and the Cape of Good Hope to trade with merchants in China, he inadvertently managed to bring the Old and New World together. Though the results of this happenstance would prove bittersweet for the experienced and knowledgeable sea captain, he achieved the goals he set for himself when he became both wealthy and famous as a result of his journey. Columbus's explorations uncovered, for his benefactors in Spain, a wealth of resources that continued to provide gold, silver, jewels, and slaves for decades, if not centuries.

Columbus was a brilliant sailor, but he was both glory- and money-hungry. He took advantage of the power bestowed upon him by the royal court of Spain. He enslaved, oversaw the torture, rape, and pillaging of most of the native cultures unfortunate enough to meet with him and his sailors, and he took advantage of the kindness and naiveté of the indigenous peoples who trusted him. On the ocean, he was a peerless navigator and mariner, but on land, he was witless, a terrible leader, and completely self-obsessed; his only motivation was to retrieve as much gold, silver, and human cargo as he could to further his own ambitions.

Knowledge that the world was round was not new in Columbus's time, but it was unknown exactly what the Earth's dimensions were. He believed, incorrectly, that there was but one ocean separating Europe from what was called the "East Indies," and that the trip between the two by sea would be fairly brief. It was later proven that his theory was incorrect when explorer Amerigo Vespucci correctly stated in his book Mundus Novus that not only were there two oceans separating Europe from Asia, but that there was a large land mass separating those two oceans.

The great paradox of Christopher Columbus is that while his "discovery" of the Americas was significant in altering the very course of history, those alterations are marked with bloodshed, misery (much of it Columbus's own), fighting, genocide, and many missed opportunities to build what could have been fair alliances with the indigenous peoples the Spanish encountered than were the conqueror-slave relationships that resulted from the heavy-handed and barbaric colonization that was imposed. Spain later learned of the grave mistakes Columbus and his men made in ignoring the long-term possibilities of the coffee bean, tobacco plants, and the hidden cities of what is now known as Central America.

Columbus did not fail to achieve his goals, but he could have achieved much more had he not been obsessed with gold, a commodity freely offered to him by the Natives, who saw no real value in it to begin with, and with further fascination with subjugating (perhaps with the intention of conversion) the people who welcomed him to their shores (at first), without fear or reservation. Had he not been possessed with the idea of finding the mythical strait to the Indian Ocean, he might have realized that he was only fifty miles from the discovery of the Pacific. His tyrannical governance of the Natives at Hispaniola and the mistreatment of the Indians on the surrounding islands prohibited the conversion of more than a few to Christianity, and he never actually set foot on the continent he was eventually credited for many centuries with discovering, save for a brief moment in Panama.

It has been said that Columbus's voyages paved the way for the transatlantic slave trade. Though slavery was not new to Europeans, Columbus's transportation of the Native islanders to Spain for the express purpose of being used as slaves paved the way for slavery to become the lucrative enterprise that it later became, as it was the Spanish settlers in the New World that declared the Natives did not "work hard enough," and that African slaves should then be imported to replace the indigenous people as they died off.

Columbus was never a friend of King Ferdinand of Spain, although Queen Isabella was a staunch supporter of the explorer. In the end, he fell out of favor with the royal court and the appointed governors sent to oversee the settlements he established, and at one point found himself bound in chains aboard a ship headed for Spain. To his great humiliation and dismay, Columbus was brought to trial for his crimes and failings as a leader on the very land he had claimed for the Spanish crown. He never fully recovered from the slight.

Nevertheless, Columbus was able to cement his name in history by being the explorer who found the route that created a permanent channel between Europe and the West. His route opened the world to the exchange of cultures, goods, services, and ideas that came to shape the world as a whole. Art, technology, education, religion, and science have all been affected and in some way influenced by the merging of the two sides of the globe brought about by Columbus's travels.

It can—and has—been said that if Columbus had not discovered the Americas, someone else would have. And while that's true, it was the spirit of adventure and the unwillingness to let imposed boundaries stop him that made Columbus unique. John Fiske said of the discoveries of Columbus that, "We shall be inclined to pronounce the voyage that led the way to this New World as the most epoch-making event of all that have occurred since the birth of Christ." Maybe not, maybe so, but either way, it can never be argued that

Christopher Columbus did not have an astounding influence on the history of navigation, exploration, colonization, and, indeed, the very Earth itself.

Chapter 1:
Early Life, and an Early Start

"You can never cross the ocean until you have the courage to lose sight of the shore."
—Christopher Columbus

Birth in Italy

Born sometime between October of either 1450 or 1451, Cristoforo Colombo, more commonly known by the name of Christopher Columbus, was born in the tiny village of Genoa. As Italy did not officially exist until March 17, 1861, throughout referred to himself his entire life as "Genoese." Genoa is now part of Italy, with close ties to Portugal. It was home to the trading cities of Seville, Barcelona, and Lisbon.

Columbus was the oldest of five children. His father, Domenico Colombo, was a weaver and tavern-keeper. His mother, Susanna Fontanarossa was the daughter of a weaver. Although it is not known whether or not Columbus received much if any formal education in his early childhood, he spoke several languages, including Portuguese, Latin, and Spanish.

Columbus is said to have been named after Saint Christopher. As the story is told, Saint Christopher was a huge man. When he heard the story of Christ, the Saint decided to search for him. A monk advised him that perhaps Christ would show himself if he were to "fast and pray." The saint refused to do so, but asked what he might do instead to meet Christ. The monk replied that he should take up residence near the strongest, most difficult river to cross in the kingdom, and devote his life to helping others cross it. Christopher agreed. He built a cabin by along the banks of the river, and used his strength to assist travelers in crossing the water by placing them on his shoulders.

One night, as he slept, he heard a child calling his name. He placed the child on his shoulders, and started across the river. Along the way, the weight of the child grew heavier and heavier, until it became almost unbearable for the giant of a man. Nevertheless, he was determined to make his way across, seeing to it that the child came to no harm. When he had finally made it to the other side, he told the child that the weight of the entire world could not have been heavier.

The child replied that he had not only borne the weight of the world on his back that night, but he had also carried the creator of the world. "I am the Christ," the child told him, "whom thou servest in doing good; and as proof of my words, plant that staff near thy cabin, and tomorrow it shall be covered with flowers and fruit." Christopher did as he was told, and the next day found that his staff had been transformed into a beautiful date tree. Undoubtedly, as his life unfolded, Christopher Columbus came to feel as though, much like his namesake, he carried the weight of the world on his own back

As a teenager, Columbus received his early business training assisting his father with the daily tasks of running the tavern, ones that often included purchasing wine and other supplies needed to run the pub. He also learned to weave. But Columbus soon grew bored with life on land, and wanted, like many of the young man in the city, to attempt to make a life as a mariner. Eventually, at the age of 14, he began working on merchant ships.

Genoa was a city of young sailors, and had built a tradition of trade with nations from as far away as the British Isles and the Mediterranean Sea. Columbus quickly became an expert sailor and navigator. He had a natural ability to determine the conditions that could arise while on the water. He was also talented at "dead reckoning," which is the ability to estimate direction and distance traveled by sea without the use of landmarks, or other methods. In spite of his youth, he was respected by his fellow sailors, and admired for his skills. His plan was to remain a merchant sailor, but an unforeseen event changed his mind, and his plans.

When Columbus was twenty-five-years-old, a merchant ship he was working on was attacked by French pirates off the coast of Portugal. In May, 1476, Columbus joined a Genoese crew that was part of a merchant convoy travelling from Portugal to England. The convoy consisted of five ships, one of which was armed. In August of that year, just off the coast of Portugal, they were attacked by a fleet of thirteen French-Portuguese war vessels. Although the convoy was commanded to surrender all five ships and all they contained to the French naval commander, Guillaume de Casenove, the Genoese refused.

In a battle that raged throughout the entire day, three of the Genoese ships and four of the French ships had been destroyed, and hundreds of men from both sides had drowned. Columbus, who had fought on one of the ships that perished, was able to catch hold of a plank of wood and float to shore. He made his way to the city of Lisbon, where his brother, Bartholomew, had become a map-maker.

While he worked as a map-maker himself for a brief time and as a sugar merchant on the islands of the coast of Africa, he became acquainted with many of the era's most famous sailors. When he returned to Lisbon, he continued to study navigation, mathematics, cartography, and astronomy. He began to examine the writings of the sailors, explorers, teachers, and philosophers who detailed their studies of the form and shape of the earth, and the best ways to traverse it by sea.

The sailors of Portugal were beginning to experiment with new forms of navigation, and to journey farther west and south than had previously been traveled by ship, utilizing their knowledge of the wind and currents. Columbus sailed with these men as far as Britain, Iceland, and Africa, although they never sailed far west on the Atlantic, as the sailors feared what might lay ahead in what they called "the sea of darkness." Columbus, however, had been reading the writings of a famed geographer from Florence named Paolo Toscanelli, who believed that the shortest route to the Far East from Europe was to sail west across the Atlantic Ocean.

Columbus and the Age of Discovery and Exploration

By the time Columbus was old enough to decide on a profession for himself, Europeans were fascinated with China and the riches it held, in part due to Marco Polo's tales of the amazing wealth, silks, jewels, spices, and customs he experienced during his travels to what was called the East Indies. Beginning in the early 1400's, Portuguese ships called caravels traveled often between Europe and the African coast, trading for spices, gold, slaves, exotic fabrics, and other desired wares. Portugal wasn't the only nation in Europe to send out expeditions of explorers with the hopes of discovering wealth and resources and claiming lands for colonization, either. Many of the European nations underwent similar efforts to expand their influence and wealth. This era of searching and exploring was called the "Age of Discovery."

Due to Spain and their mission of "Reconquista," the attempt to expel Jews and Muslims from Europe, the land route to Asia was off-limits to European travelers. Besides being an extremely long and difficult route, there was now the threat of war with the expelled factions. Muslims had control of the city of Constantinople, a necessary stop on the way to the East for supplies and rest to continue their journey. As a result, explorers were forced to sail south along the coast of Africa, around the Cape of Good Hope, and then north to China. The journey took months, and was extremely arduous. The ruling class clamored for an alternate route that would be faster and safer. Although the idea was not a new one, Columbus's theory that the shorter route to the Far East was possible became his sole focus.

Columbus theorized that the circumference of the Earth was much smaller than previously believed. He was convinced that by sailing west across the Atlantic he could reach the Far East faster, and with considerably more ease. He went to King John of Portugal and presented his plan. Not only did the king deny Columbus's request, the King then stole Columbus's idea and sent ships of his own along the route. The king's ships were unsuccessful and had to turn back, however, after they were nearly destroyed in a series of terrible storms.

While in Lisbon, Columbus married a Portuguese noblewoman named Filipa Moniz Perestrelo. The two were parents to one son, Diego. In 1485, Filipa died, and Columbus took Diego to Spain. His plan was to petition King Ferdinand and Queen Isabella of Spain for sponsorship of his proposed expedition across the Atlantic Ocean in search of a shorter water route to China. He left Diego in the Spanish countryside with monks, who agreed to educate and care for the boy while Columbus pursued what the clergy assured him was his "mission from God." He stated, in a letter to the monarchs, that he would be more than willing to sail to the Far East in service of the crown.

YOUR HIGHNESSES, as Catholic Christians and Princes who love the holy Christian faith, and the propagation of it, and who are enemies to the sect of Mahoma [Islam] and to all idolatries and heresies, resolved to send me, Cristóbal Colon, to the said parts of India to see the said princes... with a view that they might be converted to our holy faith... Thus, after having turned out all the Jews from all your kingdoms and lordships... your Highnesses gave orders to me that with a sufficient fleet I should go to the said parts of India.... I shall forget sleep, and shall work at the business of navigation, so that the service is performed.

Columbus Meets With the King and Queen

King Ferdinand of Aragon was a generally disagreeable man, and ruled with a practicality that left little room for sentiment. He was shrewd and somewhat cunning, and, in one way or another, maintained interests in most of the major kingdoms of Europe. His wife, Queen Isabella of Castile, however, was his exact opposite. It was the differences between them, it was thought, that allowed their joint rule to be so successful.

Queen Isabella was attractive, if not strikingly beautiful, with blue eyes and fierce, auburn hair. The combination made her features particularly prized in Spain, where her coloring was unusual. She was gracious, friendly, and her fair and pleasant personality commanded a respect from the members of her court, as well as her subjects, that not many kings could claim.

She shunned the frivolous and gaudy baubles and trinkets usually preferred by royalty, and allowed entertainment at court only in an effort to occupy the young men in her company so as to curb their appetites for more immoral pursuits. She was a capable stateswoman, and was never involved in a scandal of any kind.

In 1486, Columbus was finally granted an audience with the king and queen. Spanish scholars and scientists were dismissive of Columbus's math, which they were convinced was incorrect. Along with the work of Toscanelli, Columbus's estimation of the circumference of the Earth was based on Marco Polo's miscalculation of the location of Japan and Ptolemy's incorrect approximations of both the size of the earth and the size of Europe and Asia. While the court's scholars believed the Earth was 25,000 miles in circumference, Columbus believed the distance was 20,000 miles. The scholars were certain the monarchs would send the sailor away at once.

King Ferdinand did not especially care for Columbus either, but Queen Isabella was an immediate admirer of his and wanted to learn more about his ideas. Unfortunately, the country was engaged in the ongoing war with the Muslims to the east, and could not consider financing the expedition at that time. They did, however, give him a small stipend to remain in the country until they could further consider his request.

Columbus remained in for Spain seven years, selling books to make a living, while he waited for the king and queen to see him again. He was known for his persistence. While he resided in Italy, he fathered a second son, Ferdinand Columbus, with Beatriz Enrique de Harana, the daughter of a Spanish farmer. The two never married, although Columbus provided for Beatriz for the rest of her life, and left her money and property when he died. Columbus was preparing to journey to France to present his idea at court there, when fate intervened.

The Spanish had finally defeated the Moors and evicted the Jews in 1492, and the king and queen were able to give Columbus's proposal real consideration. If Columbus were successful, the Spanish would be able to secure riches and possible land that would make them equal to Portugal. Columbus also promised them he would convert other nations to Christianity. He insisted they promote him to the position of "Admiral of the Ocean Sea and Viceroy of All New Lands" as part of his deal. He also negotiated ten percent of any treasure he brought back. While they were upset at his audacity, they agreed to his terms. Columbus was, at last, able to begin his voyage across the Atlantic Ocean.

Chapter 2:
Out to Sea

"No one should fear to undertake any task in the name of our Saviour, if it is just and if the intention is purely for His holy service..."
—Christopher Columbus

1492: Columbus's First Voyage

Columbus, after many years and many supplications to the king and queen, had, at last, been granted permission and the financial backing to undertake a scouting expedition, with an armada of larger ships to follow should the maiden voyage prove successful. While he had to charter his flagship, the Santa Maria, two smaller vessels, the Pinta and the Nina were forced by the crown to travel with the convoy as a punishment to the town of Palos for an infraction of Spanish law. Columbus left the port town of Palos on August 3, 1492.

Six days later, the ships stopped in the Canary Islands, due to damages to the Pinta. Repairs to the ship took nearly four weeks, and Columbus forced the inhabitants of the islands to repair the sails of the Nina during that time. He also took the opportunity to secure supplies, food, firewood, and water for the rest of the journey. This first leg of this trip is significant in that it is the origins of Columbus's heavy-handed, strong-arm tactics in forcing Spain's subjects into labor. The Guanches of the Canary Islands were forced not only to labor on behalf of the Spanish, but they were also forced to accept Christianity.

After the repairs were completed, the expedition continued out to the open sea. Believing there was a circular pattern of wind blowing in the Atlantic that would carry his ships across the ocean and then return them home, Columbus navigated using those winds. Unfortunately, the ocean was much larger than Columbus had projected, and the journey was far longer than anticipated. The crew became frightened and disheartened, but Columbus refused to return to Spain without reaching his destination.

Columbus Reaches Land

The crew, unable to navigate the ships to return home, had no choice but to hope that Columbus's promise of land and riches would eventually come true. On October 11, 1492, the sailors began to see signs of land. The king and queen had promised to pay a reward to whomever sighted land first. Although a lookout spotted land that night, the ships made landfall the next day, on October 12, 1492, and Columbus himself took credit for being the first person to see land. He personally claimed the reward later on.

When day broke, Columbus and his men went ashore. The island was one of among a chain that has become known as the Bahamas.

Columbus named the island San Salvador. They planted a flag on the beach and claimed it for Spain. While Columbus was certain he would find the land inhabited by Chinese, he discovered the native inhabitants were Taino Indians of the Lucayo tribe. The natives of the island spoke Arawak, and grew corn, cassava, and peppers, and spun and wove cotton, made trinkets of shell, bone, and precious metals, and pearls. They also made and decorated pottery with intricate designs and drawings.

The Indians were friendly, and believed Columbus and his men were gods, and welcomed them. The Spaniards realized very quickly that the Indians were a peaceful people who had no ability to defend themselves, or to wage any kind of war. Columbus forced some of the Indians on board the Santa Maria so that they could show him where they got the gold that they so freely gave to him and his men.

The Indians took him to the island he named Hispaniola, which is modern-day Haiti.

While the expedition was at Hispaniola, where the majority of the gold was found, the Santa Maria met with an unfortunate fate. On Christmas Eve, Columbus took a break from his watch on the deck, and the Santa Maria, guided by a far less experienced sailor, ended up on a reef, where the waves bounced the ship up and down on the reef below, and destroyed the hull. The remains of the ship are still somewhere off the northern coast of Haiti. The Pinta, against Columbus's wishes, had gone on a separate expedition, and he and his men had no choice but to take everything off of the ship and place it on the shore until it could be decided what to do.

Columbus, his men, and the Indians, who had little choice, as their chief (or "cacique"), Guacanagari, had ordered them to supply both canoes and manpower, spent that Christmas floating and unloading the Santa Maria. In an attempt to console Columbus, who stood weeping at the thought of losing his flagship, Guacanagari offered to give the Spanish two large houses, and all that they would need to replace whatever losses were incurred. Columbus noted that even though unloading of the ship carried on throughout the night, not a single item was missing from the register when all was accounted for.

He said of the natives: "To such an extent are they loyal and without greed for the property of others, and that king was virtuous about all." At the same time they were helping the Spanish offload the Santa Maria, the natives, who were eager to trade for hawk bells (a piece of equipment used in falconry), showed the sailors bits of gold. The cacique himself offered Columbus "four pieces of gold as big as a man's hand" if he would set aside one of the bells for him.

After all his grief, Columbus considered the destruction of the Santa Maria to be fortuitous, as he would never have thought to remain at Hispaniola long enough to discover the amounts of gold he believed to be buried there. He certainly never thought of founding a settlement there, but the easy-going nature of the Indians coupled with the seemingly unending amounts of gold they presented him led him to believe that his destiny was unfolding according to a divine plan.

Columbus Establishes a Colony on Hispaniola

The Santa Maria was the largest of the three ships in Columbus's expedition. It was decided that the men would use the planks, wood, and fastenings from the ship to build a fort on the island, and that thirty-nine of the men and most of the provisions aboard the ship would be used to establish a small colony on Hispaniola. The fort was called La Navidad, in observance of the Christmas holiday.

While the construction of the fort took place, some of the Indians reported that the Nina was two days away from the island. The cacique provided Columbus with a canoe and a messenger to take word to the captain of the Nina, Martin Alonso, that he and Columbus should resolve their differences, and that it was in the best interest of all that the Pinta and the Nina sail home to Spain together. He did not receive word from the captain, and believed that he should depart at once, lest Alonso beat him back to Spain with news of the voyage.

The night before Columbus was to set sail for Spain, the cacique gave a feast, and was sorry to see his new "friend" leave. When Columbus and his men boarded the Nina, which had become the flagship, he found that the wind had turned directions, and that he was unable to sail. It took two full days before the Nina could set sail. After another two days of sailing, the Nina encountered the Pinta. The two captains were able to come to an agreement, and the ships traveled back to Spain together, just as they had sailed to the New World.

The Arduous Journey Home

For the first month at sea, the Nina and Pinta experienced calm waters. The weather was pleasant, and progress was steady. As the ship neared the northern Atlantic, they had no way of knowing Europe was experiencing the worst winter in decades. With winds that were extremely high and creating monstrous waves, the already travel-worn ships were tossed and rolled along the route. It was necessary to remove the sails and to let the ships be drawn with the wind. Fear, worry, and anxiety was rampant among the crews of both vessels.

Although the ships tried to keep sight of each other by using flares, they were separated by the storm. Columbus, aboard the Nina, had no idea where the Pinta was, or if she could withstand the torrential winds, rain, and waves. By the following morning, the storm began to calm. Better still, Columbus could see land. Although the sailors believed they had reached their destination, Columbus, experienced as he was on the north Atlantic, knew that they had sailed into the Azores, an island range off the coast of Portugal. He also knew that there would be trouble.

As the place where the Nina had found herself was under Portuguese control, Columbus was concerned that his expedition would be mistaken for the illegal traders who often sailed along the coast of western Africa. If he had had a choice, he would have sailed away from the islands and continued on his way to Spain. Unfortunately, the Nina was badly in need of repairs, and the men were still shaken from the storms, and they needed rest and supplies. Columbus had no choice. He devised a plan.

Sending half the crew to shore to scout for supplies, he waited aboard the Nina to see if they would be arrested. Before the men could make it to the small chapel that was their first destination, they were surrounded and taken prisoner by Portuguese men who demanded to know their business on the island. Columbus then moved the Nina to a less conspicuous waterfront, and prepared to go ashore to demand that his men be released. Fortunately, an official of the island rowed out to meet the Nina, saving Columbus the trip.

When the official demanded information regarding the ship and its mission, Columbus told him who he was, and that he was on official business for King Ferdinand and Queen Isabella, and demanded that his men be freed at once. The official did not believe him, and told him that he would still have to come ashore. Columbus refused to leave the ship, knowing he would be arrested. He threatened to have the official arrested after he returned to Spain. When the official refused to comply, the Admiral threatened to kill everyone on the island if his men were not returned.

Eventually, Columbus gave the order to his crew to move the Nina, so that they might search for provisions elsewhere. When he returned to the island two days later, the official had apparently changed his mind and released the captives. They departed without further incident.

With almost 800 miles to go before he reached Spain, Columbus ran into even more inclement weather upon leaving the Azores. It was only because of his considerable navigational skills that the ship survived long enough to reach the city of Lisbon.

Once there, Columbus met with the same issues he had experienced in the Azores. Portuguese officials in Lisbon also wanted to know why the Nina was in Portuguese waters, and whether or not illegal trading had occurred. Columbus, although he refused to leave the ship, showed them his orders from the crown of Spain, and attempted to explain that he was returning from what he still thought was the Orient. He was allowed to stay anchored until he was able to leave.

While he was in Lisbon, Columbus was invited by the King of Portugal to meet and to discuss his voyage, which the king had twice refused to finance. It is unclear exactly what took place at the meeting, but Columbus met with the Queen of Portugal to pay his respects, and to repeat his story. There were no further incidents, and he was allowed to be on his way.

Almost eight months after he had first set sail searching for a Western route to the East, Columbus arrived back in Spain.

Columbus Returns a Hero

The captain of the Pinta, who was not nearly the sailor Columbus was, had reached Spain before Columbus, which was one of Columbus's fears, however, he had drifted so far north that, even with all the delays the Nina suffered, the Pinta still arrived after Columbus had landed, made his triumphant entry, and received his hero's welcome. News of his success had traveled ahead of him, and from Palos to Barcelona and Portugal, Columbus was considered one of the great explorers of the day.

Notwithstanding the fact that he had failed to actually reach the Far East, his return with gold, pearls, spices, and natives overshadowed that small detail. Columbus felt vindicated, and was less than gracious to those who had doubted his mathematics, (although there were still correct in their doubts). Twenty years later, the expedition of Magellan proved that his calculations were off considerably. At the time of Columbus's return from his first voyage, however, it didn't seem to matter much.

He took a small group of men, dressed the six Tainos he'd brought with him from the New World in European fashion, and made his way to Barcelona, where the king and queen were holding court at the time, stopping in Cordoba to visit his sons. The king and queen, after hearing Columbus's tales and seeing the

Tainos, immediately secured the services of Pope Alexander VI to issue Spain the right to claim all lands from the west of the Azores to the Canary Islands. Although the declaration caused friction with Portugal, who was preparing to venture westward as well, the two counties later settled their differences and agreed to divide the land in the New World.

The king and queen required Columbus to immediately begin preparations for a second voyage, one meant to solely focus on colonization of the new lands. A plan was drawn, and among the chief considerations was the retrieval and distribution of gold, which would be the main motivation for colonists to leave Spain and settle in the New World. Again, Columbus demanded a percentage of all the gold he brought back to Spain. Still reluctant, the crown agreed.

Columbus was already a wealthy man. He could easily have handed the plans to younger men to continue the colonization of the New World. But Columbus was intent on converting the natives to Christianity. Nor had he given up the dream of finding the strait that would take him to the Indian Ocean and deposit him directly in the Orient. He had not forgotten that his original mission had been to find the western water route to the Far East. He prepared, once again, to cross the Atlantic.

Chapter 3:

Atrocities

"As soon as I arrived in the Indies, in the first island which I found, I took some of the natives by force, in order that they might learn and might give me information of whatever there is in these parts. And so it was that they soon understood us, and we them, either by speech or by signs, and they have been very serviceable."
—**Christopher Columbus**

Slavery in Europe in Columbus's Time

The concept of one group of people enslaving another is as old as civilization itself, and Columbus's time was no different from any other historical era. While slavery existed in northern Europe after the fall of the Roman Empire, by the 1100's, slavery was all but unheard of in the area. While it remained a common practice in southern and eastern Europe due to trade with countries across the

Mediterranean Sea, it wasn't until Portugal began experimenting with sailing techniques that allowed them to trade along the eastern coast of Africa that northern Europe saw an increase in the number of slaves transported for the sole purpose of providing free labor.

Portugal became part of a thriving Arab slave trade that was categorized as "chattel slavery," in which human beings are bought and sold as replacements for hired servants. The Portuguese realized the benefit of slave labor when the first crop of sugar cane was planted on the Portuguese island of Madeira, and slaves were captured and brought to the island to plant and harvest the crops. In 1454, the Spanish also began to import slaves from Africa.

In 1462, with the colonization of Cape Verde, a market was created for the buying and selling of slaves, and in 1470, Spanish traders began to trade and sell large groups of slaves as a commodity. During La Reconquista, a war that raged between the Spanish and the Moors for many years, slaves were taken from both sides of the conflict, and were retained by both sides when the Moors surrendered to the Spanish in 1492. While Isabella was against slave trading, it was a part of the culture she was familiar with, and she therefore allowed Columbus some leeway when it came to capturing the Indians he met in the New World.

The Spanish Atrocities Committed Against the Indians

While the first voyage to the New World was entirely devoted to exploration and the discovery of a new trade route, the encounter with the indigenous people of what became known as the Bahamas, the Caribbean Islands, Cuba, Jamaica, and Hispaniola (Haiti and the

Dominican Republic), and, to a lesser extent, Panama, Columbus and his crew unwittingly opened the door to what became a centuries-long tradition of transatlantic slave trading. First, it was used as a means of securing translators and workers, and later as the pillar of an economic system that would not have been able to exist without the capture and subjugation beginning with Native Americas, and then Africans.

When Columbus discovered there was gold to be had in the New World, he immediately faced the problem of how to retrieve it from the earth. Lacking the manpower, the tools, or the knowledge to recover precious metals or to dive and extract pearls, the friendly, giving nature of the Indians unfortunate enough to cross paths with the Spanish became their undoing. Columbus quickly went from explorer to conquistador. He said, upon meeting the Taino for the first time: "These people are very unskilled in arms... with 50 men they could all be subjected and made to do all that one wished."

When Columbus encountered a new tribe, he captured several members in order to teach them Spanish, so that they could serve as translators. These captives were held on the ships, where many suffered horribly at the hands of the Spanish sailors. Columbus, devout Christian that he was, saw no wrongdoing in trading or buying and selling young girls as though they were property. He wrote in his journal concerning the proclivities of his men. "A hundred castellanoes are as easily obtained for a woman as for a farm, and it is very general and there are plenty of dealers who go about looking for girls; those from nine to ten are now in demand."

A friend of Columbus, Michael da Cuneo, who was aboard one of the ships, related an incident that describes the relationship between the natives and the Spanish at that time.

While I was in the boat, I captured a very beautiful Carib woman, whom the said Lord Admiral gave to me. When I had taken her to my cabin she was naked—as was their custom. I was filled with a desire to take my pleasure with her and attempted to satisfy my desire. She was unwilling, and so treated me with her nails that I wished I had never begun. But—to cut a long story short—I then took a piece of rope and whipped her soundly, and she let forth such incredible screams that you would not have believed your ears. Eventually we came to such terms, I assure you, that you would have thought that she had been brought up in a school for whores.

This account symbolizes both the rape of an Indian woman and foretells the atrocities that eventually befell the Indians on the islands under the command of Columbus and his men for more than a decade.

Columbus not only allowed his men to commit unspeakable crimes against the native population, but often demanded "punishments" be meted out due to whatever infraction he deemed deserving. On command, Indians who did not obey the orders of the Spanish, or who simply resisted the usurpation of their homes, food, goods, and land were attacked with Spanish war dogs, weapons, and canons, among other forms of torture. The priest Bartolomé de Las Casas said of the torture inflicted upon the Indians that the Spanish "thought nothing of knifing Indians by the tens and twenties and of cutting slices off them to test the sharpness of their blades."

It was also during this era of forced labor that Columbus instituted quotas for the amounts of gold he required from the Indians monthly.

Every Indian aged 14 and older was required to collect gold for the Spanish. There were severe punishments, including severing hands and ears, for failing to meet the quotas. Unfortunately for the natives, there was far less gold to be found than Columbus originally expected, and it was not long before the Indians were unable to meet the quotas at all. Mass suicides took place among the Indians as a result of the life they were forced to endure.

Columbus captured nearly one thousand Tainos, and after selecting the best 500 men, women, and children to send to the slave market in Seville, he allowed his men to do whatever they wished with those who remained. Those natives who were undesirable to the Spanish were allowed to flee to the far reaches of the islands to live the rest of their lives as best they could manage. Of the 500 Taino sent to Seville, only 250 survived the journey. The rest died en route.

When Columbus had set out on his second journey, one of his intentions was to convert the natives to Christianity. However, since workers were needed to secure the gold that ultimately became his overruling obsession, he discarded his noble mission of saving souls and became more interested in procuring goods from those he initially sought to save. Since the crown had decreed Spanish citizens could not be enslaved, and since those living in lands claimed for Spain automatically became Spanish citizens, Columbus solved his dilemma by refusing to baptize the natives on Hispaniola and the other islands. Baptism was a requirement for citizenship, as Spain was a staunchly Catholic nation at the time. Since they were not citizens, Columbus was able to exploit these people freely.

The Indians Columbus encountered were Lucayans, Tainos, and Arawaks. It was the Arawaks who had helped the Spanish unload the Santa Maria after it was shipwrecked during the first voyage. Two years after Columbus landed, 125, 000 of them—half the indigenous population—were dead.

Before Columbus sailed west and "discovered" the New World, the population of Hispaniola was upwards of one million. By 1542, the population had been depleted to around 200 indigenous people living on the island. By 1555, the population of Arawak had been completely destroyed. Not all of the deaths were due to slaughter by the soldiers or suicide. Many of the natives contracted small pox, tuberculosis, diphtheria, measles, typhus, influenza, and other diseases, against which they had no immunities.

Christopher Columbus and the Legacy of Slavery

In all, Columbus was responsible for the transatlantic transport of nearly 5,000 slaves during his time as an explorer and conqueror. Beginning with the Arawak and culminating in the transportation of slaves from the western coast of Africa, the slave trade, although not a new undertaking in Europe and the Mediterranean, became a viable, economic industry thanks in part to Columbus's use of slaves to enhance the wealth of Spain. His personal fortune was greatly enhanced by the selling of slaves as well.

Another motivation for Columbus to enslave the Taino was to ensure that he would be able to repay debts to the crown should he not find the treasures he hoped to find in the Orient. Though he sailed from one island to the next, always believing he would find the straight that would take him to China, Columbus knew that he would surely be able to at least see some profit from the sale of the Tainos.

When it became undeniable that there was enough gold to satisfy the greed of the Spanish conquerors, a plantation system was instituted, called the ecomienda system. For those Spanish who owned large plots of land, the Indians were forced to work as farmers and servants. The Indians were also subjected to sexual slavery, and were often bought and sold solely for that purpose.

With the indigenous people of the Indies dying at accelerated rates, the Spanish realized they would need to replace their workforce. With the depletion of stores of precious metals and the consumption of easily harvested foods, the plantation system of agriculture spread throughout not only the islands, but made its way to the continent of America. Slavery proved to be a very way to dramatically improve profits.

Columbus and his men set a precedent that was followed by conquerors and explorers from Europe for centuries to come in the quest to acquire lands and wealth for themselves. The 1519 campaign of terror, torture, and slaughter waged by Hernán Cortes against the Aztec empire was modeled after Columbus's actions on the island of Hispaniola years earlier, and the Inca of Peru suffered much the same fate at the hands of Francisco Pizarro.

Trading posts along the coast of Western Africa initially meant for the trade of goods became markets for the trading, purchase, and sale of human beings as property. Along with the abduction of Africans from the coasts and raids conducted in villages in the interior of Africa by slave traders, the growth of the industry led to the creation of the Middle Passage, the route taken by slave traders from the coast of Africa to the Americas.

While the ongoing wars between Christians and Muslims produced many slaves of heritages other than African—mostly Russians or Arabs—Europeans had learned, by the time Columbus had sailed to the New World, that it was cheaper and easier to buy and export slaves from Africa, with whom Portugal had already established relationships.

Due to the favorable currents and easy access to many different coastlines, the Middle Passage became the favored transportation route for slavers. The fact that African slaves were born and raised in much the same conditions as the Indians and utilized many of the same mining, agricultural, and farming practices made them ideal replacements for the rapidly diminishing indigenous population.

Much as the Tainos were shipped to the slave market in Seville by Columbus, so African slaves were shipped, under deplorable conditions, to slave markets from South America to the Eastern coast of what became the Unites States of America. Slaves endured voyages of two to four months in the holds of ships, with unbearably extreme temperatures, chained together much as animals and cargo during transit, African slaves were forced to exist on little to no food, with very little breathable air, while also being forced to lie in one another's excrement. Like the Tainos before them, many did not survive the journey.

Between the years of 1492, when the first Indian slaves were shipped to Seville, to 1505, when the first African slaves were shipped to Hispaniola, and 1888, when slavery was officially abolished in Brazil, the transatlantic slave trade was responsible for tens of millions of lost and stolen lives. The cultures, customs, histories, and legacies of indigenous and African peoples have been lost, stolen, altered, and shattered by the greed, cruelty, and heartlessness of those who placed wealth and power above the rights of other human beings.

While slavery in and of itself is as old as man's ability to conquer and subjugate one another, slavery as an industry began with Columbus's voyage to the New World. The slave trade, as utilized by Christopher Columbus during his travels in the Americas, provided both Europe and the Americas with continuous free labor for generations, and made possible the continued oppression, exploitation, and marginalization of the poor, indigenous, and disenfranchised. This is the dark side of the legacy of Christopher Columbus.

Chapter 4:

The Second Journey

"Nothing that results in human progress is achieved with unanimous consent. Those that are enlightened before the others are condemned to pursue that light in spite of the others."
—Christopher Columbus

The Second Voyage: 1493

The crown dispatched Columbus on his second voyage to the New World with strict orders to establish the largest colony in the West, up to that time. Although the Portuguese had established colonies along the western coast of Africa, the king and queen of Spain resolved to surpass their European neighbors. It was naturally necessary for those inhabitants of the New World who were to become Spanish subjects to be converted and baptized into the Christian faith. Columbus took that mission to heart as his divine calling.

On September 25, 1493, Columbus began his second voyage. Ferdinand and Isabella this time equipped him with 17 ships, and somewhere between 1,000 and 1,500 men. The would-be colonists brought mainly tradesman, laborers, and the tools and supplies needed to build a legitimate colony in the New World. One passenger counted among them was a very young Ponce de Leon, who later accomplished a feat Columbus was never able to claim: he actually became the first Spaniard to set foot on soil in the continental United States. As Columbus had greatly exaggerated his tales of the riches and easy living in "The Indies," many of the contingent were set on achieving great wealth with little effort.

Stopping, just as he had during the first voyage, in the Canary Islands, the convoy was able to stock the ships with provisions and to prepare for the journey with no interference from the Portuguese. The journey to Guanahani was largely uneventful, and although his destination was La Navidad, Columbus sailed further south to make landfall on an island called "Caire" by the Indians, but which Columbus named "Dominica." The island is part of a chain that is now among American territories.

Columbus intended to go ashore and claim the land for Spain, just as he had with San Salvador during his first voyage. However, he was met with a very different type of native. Columbus encountered, for the first time, Caribs. They were not as friendly as the Tainos, nor were they as eager to share their wares. They were better equipped to defend themselves, having possession of bows and arrows, along with crude (but effective) knives. The clashes began as soon as the Spanish landed. It was during his brief skirmish, which ended after the death of one Carib and the serious injury of another. The Caribs capitulated and were subjugated, but were never baptized. This demonstrates that Columbus's intended objective to convert the "heathens" almost immediately gave way to his obsession with finding wealth.

The expedition sailed further south and landed on the island of Santa Cruz. Upon their approach to the shore, the Spanish were surprised by an attack from the Caribs, who were just as surprised to see the Spanish on their shores. Two of the Spanish were injured in the brief skirmish. There was a Carib aboard one of the ships that had been captured who was pronounced too badly injured in his fight with the Spanish to live long. In a show of strength to the Caribs who were attacking from the shore, Columbus ordered the Carib thrown into the bay.

Unfortunately, the Carib man did not die, and began to swim toward the shore. Warned by the Tainos aboard the ship that the Caribs would attack in full force should he make it to shore, the Christians pulled the man back into the boat, bound his hands and legs, and pitched him back into the water. Remarkably, the man somehow managed to free himself and again swam for shore. The Spaniards then filled him with arrows until, at last, he sank for good. Several of the Caribs on shore attempted to swim to the boats to attack, but were slaughtered long before they could prove a real threat. It has been said that this unwarranted killing of the Caribs, especially considering that the ships could easily have sailed on and left them in peace, was the act that angered God, and turned Him against the Admiral.

The fleet left Santa Cruz and sailed to the Virgin Islands, so named by Columbus after Saint Ursula. The ships sailed past Puerto Rico and stopped to replenish their water supply along the southern shore of the island. The natives, no doubt warned by their neighbors to avoid the strangers at all costs, ran and hid at the ships' approach, and were able to evade the exploring party that Columbus sent out. There were no slaves taken, no rapes committed, and no murders during this layover. Guided by the Tainos aboard, he sailed until he reached the eastern tip of Hispaniola, and had returned to familiar waters. He continued on his way to La Navidad.

After signaling to the fort from sea the night before and receiving no response, Columbus decided to wait until the following morning to go ashore. The next morning, he found that the fort was gone, and all of the settlers had been killed by the natives. The killings, of course had been in response to the Spanish treatment of the Indians. Since there was not nearly as much gold on Hispaniola as Columbus thought, the settlers left behind had become angry and discontented with the fact that they were not getting rich.

Running out of food and supplies, as the natives died of measles and smallpox among other diseases brought to the islands by the Spanish, the settlers who had been left behind to govern the settlement had, in Columbus's absence, begun raiding villages, stealing gold, women, children, and food from the Indians. The Spanish were also dying, many from syphilis, which they contracted from the natives.

A Taino chief by the name of Caonabo had decided he'd had enough, and began killing the Spanish one at a time, until the original number of 39 had diminished enough for the rest to be killed in one attack. When Columbus returned and was told of the events that had occurred, a cousin of Guacanagari, the chief who had befriended Columbus during his first journey, explained that they had attempted to stop the revolt, but that they were unable to do so. The cacique, the cousin explained, had been injured in the attempt, and was unable to personally meet with the Admiral.

In the days following his arrival at La Navidad, Columbus realized he may have misjudged the meekness and compliance of the Tainos. He also decided that he should find a safer place to settle his next colony. He set sail along the shore of Haiti, and after three weeks and nearly thirty-two miles, he selected a site along the northern coast of the Dominican Republic. He named the new settlement La Isabela. While the colonists began to set up their new life, disappointment and unease had already began to creep in among the assemblage, who were beginning to realize life in the New World was not going to be as easy or as lucrative as they had been led to believe.

Columbus Establishes More Settlements

Columbus sent two groups further inland of La Isabela to explore the Cibao, which was the name of the valleys and mountain ranges of the island. The groups came back with small amounts of gold dust, but only what they had been able to trade for with the Tainos. While it may have been better for Columbus to wait until he had actually found real riches, he sent twelve of his ships back to Cadiz to report to the king and queen that he was achieving his directives, and also to request more men and supplies.

Due to the fact that the ships Columbus sent back held two dozen Tainos to be sold at the slave market in Seville, along with what gold he had been able to secure from the Tainos, the royals granted his requests, still unaware of the massacre at La Navidad. Unfortunately, things were not going well for the men at La Isabela, who, unaccustomed to the harsh living conditions and tropical diseases of the Caribbean, were sick and dying. Mutinous plots were beginning to take shape.

In order to quiet the growing unhappiness within his crew, Columbus gathered a group of skilled laborers and led them into the Cibao to construct an inland fort. Along the way, the men traded with the Tainos for gold, food, and other charms, taking by force what they wanted when their requests were refused. Those Taino with enough foresight to lock up and leave their homes in advance of the march were rewarded when Columbus ordered their homes left untouched. Bizarrely, though he allowed the rape, murder, and subjugation into slavery of the natives, Columbus did not disturb a single home that was unoccupied.

Columbus's choice of the Greater Antilles to house the fort was a fortuitous one, for there was more gold at the site than he had found up to that point. The Tainos continued to supply the Spanish with gold, and unlike at La Navidad, there was no need to institute quotas, or to force labor. His biggest problem was preventing the men from trading privately with the Indians. He was forced to decree that any colonist caught trading privately with the Indians would be whipped, or worse.

Seventeen days after the march began, Columbus left the men at the new fort, called Santo Tomás, and returned to La Isabella. Although the ground was yielding better crops than the soil at La Navidad and the men were in no immediate danger of starvation, the colonists were impatient to see more gold. Columbus sent some of the men to Santo Tomás to relieve the men there. He prayed that the supply ships would return from Spain in time to prevent another revolt. He also sent out another exploratory group.

The explorers encountered a small group of Tainos that had managed to steal some of the Spaniards' clothing. They swiftly rounded up the Indians and cut the ears off of one of the men. The rest were taken to Columbus, who immediately ordered them beheaded. Despite most of the Taino aiding the Spaniards, he had no problem sentencing them to execution. A cacique from a nearby settlement pleaded with Columbus for the Indians' lives, and Columbus reconsidered, but the damage had been done. The Tainos were finally beginning to see the Spanish were not their friends in any way.

Columbus in Cuba and Jamaica

Though he was satisfied with the progress of the two settlements on Hispaniola, Columbus was aware by that time that he was not in Asia. He returned to the sea to continue his search for the Strait of India. He found himself in Cuba, where the Taino there told him he could find more gold on an island to the south. Columbus named the island Santiago, but the Indians called it Jamaica. The Tainos on Jamaica, however, were not as friendly as their Cuban counterparts, and they met the expedition with seventy canoes en route to meet the ships in the water. Unwilling to be diplomatic, Columbus fired canons at the canoes, slaughtering many of them.

The following day, Tainos threw spears and stones, and aimed bows and arrows at the

Spanish, who retaliated by unleashing a Spanish war dog. The dog, the likes of which had never been seen by the Indians, killed several of the Tainos. The Spanish also sent crossbowmen, who killed another seventeen of the Indians. The rest retreated, and the expedition came ashore. The ships were docked for four days, during which the subdued Indians came forward to give the Spanish fish and fruit in exchange for hawk bells and beads. Fortunately for all involved, there was no gold to be found, making further violence unnecessary.

Columbus sailed along the coast of Cuba, and eventually made the decision to turn and sail back the way he'd come. Had he continued along the route he had taken, he would have made it to the Yucatan, where he would, indeed, have found the lost cities that contained more gold, jewels, and wealth than he could have imagined. Unfortunately for him, he never knew this, and did not recover those riches for himself. The return trip to La Isabela took three months.

Columbus and His Brothers in the New World

When Columbus returned to La Isabela, he was pleased to find his youngest and favorite brother, Bartholomew, had come from Spain on one of the supply ships, which had arrived in his absence. Recovering from an illness he'd contracted while exploring Cuba and Jamaica, he was relieved to know his brother, who had helped him conceive the original journey, was by his side. Unfortunately, Columbus had left his other brother, Diego, in charge of the colony at La Isabela while he was off exploring, and things had deteriorated badly under his leadership.

Diego had been left with strict orders not to pillage, rape, or punish the Tainos, except for in cases of theft. One of Columbus's lieutenants, Pedro Margarit, took nearly four hundred men on what was supposed to be an exploratory mission. The men took neither provisions nor food with them, and soon had to resort to ransacking and looting the Indians' homes as a result of their lack of foresight. They stole what gold they found, and ate all of the Tainos food stores, leaving them with no food for themselves. The Christians raped many Taino women and girls, and kidnapped Taino children to sell into slavery.

When Diego attempted to stop Margarit, the lieutenant and his gang instead commandeered one of the relief ships and sailed back to Spain. Those men who remained split into several groups and continued to pillage the island. Some of the Taino tried to fight back, with little success. Columbus's solution, upon his arrival, was to unleash his men on the Taino, who were hunted down and rounded up. In spite of all that the Taino had done for the Spanish, Columbus, once again, turned on the friendly Indians who had provided him with so much.

When he had the surviving Taino brought to the center of the fort, he selected the 500 best, those he deemed most desirable, to send to the slave market in Seville. The rest were either allowed to flee or given to his men to do with as they wished. Order was temporarily restored. Unfortunately, all the gold the rogue factions had extorted or stolen from the Indians was hidden in their private stashes, and Columbus was left with nothing to send the crown except human cargo.

The king and queen of Spain were against the transportation of the Indians to Seville, and had ordered there be no further slaving until the matter could be discussed with Columbus in a face-to-face meeting, but the Admiral felt he had no choice but to send the captured Tainos back, as he had nothing else. The royals allowed the 250 Indians who survived the journey to be sold, but they did not forget that he had disobeyed their orders.

Columbus's next move was to capture the still-at-large Taino chief, Caonabo, who was responsible for the massacre at La Navidad. When both Caonabo and his brother-in-law had been captured and imprisoned at La Isabela, any resistance from the Indians was quelled, and order was temporarily restored once more. Columbus and his brothers established three more forts in Hispaniola, and reinstated gold quotas for every Taino over the age of fourteen. Conditions on Hispaniola further deteriorated for the natives, despite the already dismal welfare.

When four more supply ships arrived from Spain, the commander of the fleet was Juan Aguando, who had sailed with Columbus to the New World during the second journey, but who had returned to Spain earlier. Aguando was sent by the crown to observe the conditions on the island, as negative reports had begun to reach the court. He ordered his men to document the daily events that took place on Hispaniola, and found that almost all of the colonists desired to return to Spain. Columbus knew his second return to Spain would necessitate answers to charges of greed leveled by both Margarit, who was already on his way, and Juan Aguando. He prepared to leave for Spain, but was delayed by a hurricane that destroyed three of his ships.

Before he departed, Columbus left orders with Diego and Bartholomew to build a better colony than La Isabela, and the two constructed Santo Domingo from the wreckage of the ships destroyed by the hurricane. The city is, today, the capital of the Dominican Republic, and is the oldest European city in the Western Hemisphere. La Isabela, abandoned shortly after construction began, became a ruin. They can still be visited today.

When Columbus began his second return trip to Spain in March of 1496, he had been in the New World for two and a half years. He carried with him thirty Tainos to present to the royal court, and his ships were dangerously battered, overcrowded, and damaged. The sailors were disillusioned, half-starved, and financially broke, as the riches and gold they were promised were not obtained, and many were gravely ill. These realities, when compared to the exaggerated stories of untold riches and easy living used to convince people to sail with him on the second journey had badly damaged Columbus's reputation, and ensured that he would have many questions to answer once he finally arrived in Spain.

Chapter 5:
A Shattered
Reputation

"I should be judged as a captain who went from Spain to the Indies to conquer a people numerous and warlike, whose manners and religion are very different from ours, who live in sierras and mountains, without fixed settlements, and where by divine will I have placed under the sovereignty of the King and Queen our Lords, an Other World, whereby Spain, which was reckoned poor, is become the richest of countries. Columbus is coming from the Indies as a prisoner to Cadiz."

—Christopher Columbus

Columbus Faces the Royal Court

When Columbus finally reached Seville, he visited the archbishop, Andrés Bernáldez. He knew that his return to the royal court would be filled with questions and accusations. He was aware of the court's displeasure not only because of the continued enslavement of

Indians in the New World without the crown's permission, but also due to the reported treatment of Spanish colonists under Columbus's terrible governorship. He knew the trip from Seville to the town where the royal court was being held was his only chance to turn public sentiment back in his favor.

As he had for his return from the first journey, Columbus dressed the natives in bright, gaudy costumes, and brought along exotic birds, golden masks and trinkets, and the Indians' feathered headdresses to exhibit in the small towns along the way to meet with the king and queen. Columbus's son, Ferdinand, was had become a page to Queen Isabella, and he may have been able to speak positively of his father's return, paving the way for his father to be received with grace by the monarchs.

Evidently, the grand display Columbus was able to put on impressed the king and queen enough that his arrival at court was, in fact, a positive—if not entirely celebratory—event. The claims of the sailor's detractors were largely dismissed when the Admiral was able to present the royal court with proof of what appeared to be his most successful expedition yet. The promise of more gold, land, and power for Spain caused the royals to turn a blind eye to Columbus's crimes during his leadership. They consented to a third journey.

The purpose of the third voyage was to assist the colonies and to continue to explore the west. Despite his previous failures, Columbus was still intent on finding the new route to China. During his second voyage, he had also come to realize that to the south of the islands there was a land mass of considerable size. In his journal, he wrote, "I have come to believe that this is a mighty continent which was hitherto unknown. I am greatly supported in this view by reason of this great river, and by this sea, which is fresh." He persuaded the royals to let him explore it and claim it for Spain.

While Columbus may have managed to placate the crown, tales of the horrors of life in the New World had become common knowledge. It was extremely difficult to convince the Spanish that sailing with him to the Indies would be beneficial to anyone other than Columbus, himself. The Admiral's greed and lust for gold had become legendary. This had caused many of the professional sailors and potential colonists to decline joining his next voyage.

In order to ensure Columbus would have enough Spaniards to create more colonies, the king and queen offered to pardon those convicted of minor crimes such as prostitution, debtors, petty thieves, and similarly non-violent charges. Women were also allowed, for the first time, to travel with the third expedition, which many hoped would prevent further cases of rape among the natives, and to also encourage the establishment of communities in the new colonies. Furthermore, should they survive their time in the New World and return to Spain, the would-be colonists were promised a stipend, and amnesty upon their return.

Columbus was granted six ships in all, with two sent ahead of the actual expedition. After nearly two years of delays, he finally began his third voyage to the New World. Believing there was more gold to the south of his earlier landings, and still set on fining his way to Asia, he planned the third voyage with a more southerly route. He was sure there were more islands south of the Lesser Antilles that would provide him with more wealth, even if that meant subduing more natives as slaves. His objective to convert the natives was becoming less and less important.

The expedition stopped, once again, at the Canary Islands and the Cape Verde Islands before undertaking the transatlantic crossing. As the winds died for days, leaving the ships adrift with little forward motion, the supplies began to spoil, and casks of wine began to burst open from the heat. Finally, near the end of July, the winds picked up, and the convoy was able to make progress. The passengers, who were already dubious about the journey, began to mumble amongst themselves that perhaps they had made the wrong choice. Columbus was aware of their discontent, and his health was also declining.

Ironically, while Columbus was still determined to find a westward route to Asia, explorer Vasco de Gama was establishing an eastern sea route that eventually became the route most used by Europeans in their dealings with Asia. The new sea route was shorter, and much less arduous than the previous one.

Columbus was unaware of this development, as he was preoccupied with both his health and the growing unease of the crew and passengers aboard his ships.

Columbus Explores South America and Returns to Chaos on Hispaniola

Columbus had sent three of the ships from the Canary Islands directly to Hispaniola, while he remained with the rest in order to explore the more southern route he had in mind. He docked in Trinidad, and were met by Carib Indians, who, although they initially attacked them, became friendly toward the expedition. After a small amount of trading took place, they set sail for the coast of what is now Venezuela. Because he had an eye infection at the time, Columbus did not leave his ship, and never made it to land in South America.

Upon further shipboard exploration, he realized he had reached what he called an "other world," which he believed may be the literal Garden of Eden. He did not, however, stop to explore the land on foot, as his brothers, who remained at Santo Domingo, were in desperate need of supplies and help. The ships he had dispatched from the Canaries, manned and captained by sailors who were not as capable at sea as their Admiral, had become lost, and did not make it to Hispaniola until after Columbus.

On his way north, Columbus and his crew anchored along the shores of Trinidad. The natives he encountered there had never seen copper, and freely traded with Columbus for gold. As was his custom, he captured several of the Indians, who were not Tainos, so that he could teach them Spanish and use them as interpreters. There were those among the expedition who viewed Columbus's tactic of promising the Indians safety upon the approach of the ships, only to have them chained and taken captive, as a mortal sin. Columbus's reputation was eroding further still.

Having difficulty navigating many of the straits leading through the southernmost islands from South America back to the Caribbean, Columbus ignored the direction of the Indians aboard the ship that would have taken them to a seabed full of pearls. A sailor with the expedition later doubled back to retrieve those pearls, and the accusation that Columbus was holding out and attempting to keep the pearls for himself later became part of the report detailing Columbus's wrongdoings to the crown in Spain. While the accusation was untrue—Columbus simply decided to ignore the directions of the Indians in an effort to reach Hispaniola and his brothers—the story did not help his situation any.

What Columbus discovered upon his arrival in Santo Domingo was a scene of utter chaos and destruction. Spanish infighting and hostilities toward the Indians had turned the city into a complete horror. Aside from the violence, disease and hunger were rampant in the town. Columbus attempted to fix things, but, as always, proved to be ineffective as a leader on land. Of the Spanish settlers, many of the poorer ones had to resort to working the land of the wealthier settlers, because so many of the natives had died that they were running out of workers. Many of those settlers had been noblemen in Spain, and found life in the colonies unbearable.

While Santo Domingo was a much more accommodating site than La Isabela, the settlers were still mostly unhappy with their way of life in the New World. Francisco Rolodán, who had been named a high-ranking officer by Columbus before the Admiral had departed for

Spain, was attempting to organize a revolt among the colonists. Francisco knew that the reports being sent to Spain would cause the crown to eventually call Columbus's position into question, and may even remove the Admiral from power. Rolodán was attempting to secure the position of governor of Santo Domingo for himself.

While Bartholomew and Diego managed to keep Rolodán and his troupe of rebels out of the city of Santo Domingo, the Spaniards freely roamed the islands, raping, robbing, and torturing Indians with abandon. Even so, the seventy men were able to form an alliance with Indians on the far side of the island. Bartholomew was able to bring the natives under submission with terrible tactics, including burning down their villages, but he was unable to stop Rolodán and his men. By the time Columbus had returned, the state of affairs at Santo Domingo included a rogue faction terrorizing the island, down-trodden and beaten Natives, and many of the remaining Spaniards at the fort suffering from advanced stages of syphilis.

Unfortunately for Columbus, the three ships he'd sent ahead to Hispaniola made landfall near Rolodán's camp. For whatever reason, the newly-arrived reinforcements were more than happy to join the rebels in an attempt to attack the fort at Santo Domingo. Columbus, seeing the situation quickly getting out of hand, sent two of his ships back to Spain with reports of his findings in Trinidad and Venezuela, in an attempt to get ahead of the bad news he knew would surely reach the crown at some point, and to request new, dependable settlers, as he had lost so many men to the rebellion.

Columbus then sent word to Rolodán to request a meeting. He offered the rebels the choice of either returning to Spain with the gold and slaves they had captured, or ceasing the rebellion and returning to their lives at Santo Domingo with no punishment. When Rolodán demanded a monetary settlement, Columbus agreed. However, he found himself unable to pay the amount by the seven-week due date, and the two factions arrived at an impasse.

The Columbus Brothers Are Arrested

Because Columbus had also requested a judicial official be sent from Spain, the crown sent Francisco de Bobadilla as a royal commissioner, granting him the power to judge all Spanish inhabitants on the island—including Columbus and his brothers—to investigate the situation. When Bobadilla arrived on Santo Domingo, his first sight upon his arrival was of seven Spanish rebels hanging from gallows. This was Columbus's attempt to put down Rolodán and his men once and for all, but it was also the act that led to Columbus and his brothers being arrested for acting against citizens of Spain.

Bobadilla first lowered the tax on gold in order to win the favor of the colonists, and then arrested Columbus and his brothers. He had them placed in chains, and ordered their return to Spain to stand trial. In early October of 1500, the three men were placed on a ship bound for Spain. Although he was told he could take the chains off once he was aboard the ship, Columbus opted to keep them on, asserting that only Queen Isabella could remove his chains. It was ironic that he returned to Spain a prisoner aboard a Spanish ship, as had so many of the Natives he'd captured.

While the Columbus brothers had failed magnificently to govern the colonies in

Hispaniola, they were ill-equipped and not at all prepared to manage so many men in the face of gold fever, greed, and unchecked sexual domination over the non-aggressive and all but defenseless Indians. With their mother country so far away, it was almost inevitable that the situation would grow beyond their capability to control it.

But more worrisome to Columbus was the fact that he had knowingly continued to engage in slave-trading, a practice that Queen Isabella, his most loyal supporter, was against almost from the beginning. Columbus knew that, unlike his previous return to Spain, he would not have the opportunity to prepare a grand showcase of his accomplishments. He was returning to Spain in chains, disgraced and at risk of losing his freedom, his titles, his wealth, and possibly his life.

Chapter 6:
Final Voyage

> *"I came to serve you at the age of 28 and now I have not a hair on me that is not white, and my body is infirm and exhausted. All that was left to me and my brothers has been taken away and sold, even to the cloak that I wore, without hearing or trial, to my great dishonor."*
> —Christopher Columbus

Voyage Four—1502

When Columbus arrived in Spain, he went to Seville to live in a monastery. He was kept under guard, and was only able to survive due to the generosity of the resident monks. He remained there for six weeks, until Queen Isabella sent for him, and provided the funds needed for his journey to meet with the royal court. That December, Columbus and his brothers finally appeared before the royals to plead their case. He represented himself and his brothers so well that the king and queen reinstated his titles, and continued his stipend.

He had, however, lost his right to govern, and the colonies at Hispaniola came under control of a succession of governors appointed by the crown—the first of whom was Francisco de Bobadilla, the very man who had sent Columbus to Spain in chains.

At this point, Columbus was in extremely poor health. Isabella freed him and his brothers, but he had fallen out of favor with the people, as well as with King Ferdinand, who was never as enamored with Columbus as the queen was to begin with. During his time in Spain, he was able to convince the queen to force Bobadilla to take an accounting of all of his remaining holdings in the New World. The crown allowed Columbus to send a representative to Santo Domingo to secure his wealth, and to bring it back to Spain.

Columbus could have (and perhaps should have) retired from sea life to live out the rest of his days in comfort, but that was not what he did. He was still as determined to make it to China as he'd ever been. Along with his determination to secure the western trade route, his fervor to convert the native inhabitants of the New World had returned with a vengeance. Perhaps the influence of the monks in Seville had reinvigorated his sense of righteousness. It took nearly two years to convince the crown to allow him a fourth journey.

In 1502, his request was granted, and he was given four old, shabby ships (which he had to pay for himself) and sent on his way with both the blessing and the funding of the queen. The stated objective was solely the conversion of natives. Her only edict was that there be absolutely no slaving on this journey. There were 140 mostly teenage boys onboard the ships, but no colonists. In May of that year, Columbus embarked on his fourth and final journey to the Americas. His younger son, Ferdinand, along with Columbus's reluctant brother, Bartholomew, sailed with him.

The journey, unlike the previous crossings, took only three weeks to complete. He spent some time sailing around the Lesser Antilles, but made plans to dock at Santo Domingo when he realized a hurricane was approaching. As he had been ordered by the king and queen to stay away from Santo Domingo, he was disobeying by attempting to anchor there, but the severity of the impending storm caused him to risk angering the crown.

He asked the new Governor, Nicolás de Ovando, for permission to dock, but was denied. The governor was about to send thirty ships home to Spain, but Columbus warned him not to, because of the hurricane. The governor laughed and mocked him, and sent the ships out to sea anyway. One of those ships was carrying gold meant for Columbus, and another was carrying Francisco Bobadilla. The Admiral was unable to find another place to dock before the hurricane arrived, but he and his crew did their best, using his knowledge of the tropical storm systems to secure the ships. Of the thirty ships de Ovando sent to Spain, all but two were destroyed. One of the surviving vessels carried Columbus's gold. Bobadilla did not survive. Columbus's ships, by contrast, made it through the storm mostly intact.

Columbus Sails to Central America

Unwanted and unwelcome in Santo Domingo, Columbus and his crew of teenagers sailed northwest to Honduras. In August of 1452, he landed in what is now Central America, which he believed to be part of a chain of small islands off the coast of China. Unbeknownst to him, he was, once again, only miles away from the great so-called "Lost Cities" of the region, which contained all the treasures Columbus sought and more, but the native peoples, perhaps due to shared knowledge of Spanish cruelty and greed in the past, never told him of these cities. When he was unable to persuade the Honduran people to show him where he could find gold, silver, or any of the other natural resources he wanted, he moved on.

Turning south instead of continuing west, Columbus sailed along what was called the "Mosquito Coast," sparing Mexican natives the horror of meeting the Spanish for several years. After nearly three months of extremely difficult sailing, Columbus finally reached what is now known as Costa Rica, and docked at Puerto Limon. He encountered more natives there, the Talamancans, who lived around what is now called Panama.

According to the journal of Ferdinand Columbus, after a brief skirmish with the Spanish, the Talamancan chief, wishing to make amends, sent one eight-year-old and one fourteen-year-old girl to the ship as a peace offering. Aware of the danger the young girls faced at the hands of the crew, Columbus showed uncharacteristic mercy. He ordered the girls dressed, adorned with jewels, and returned to their homes unharmed. This single act of kindness on behalf of Columbus enabled the crew to go ashore for a scouting expedition a week later.

The Spanish primarily found wildlife when they ventured further inland. Although Columbus had captured one of the Talamancans to serve as an interpreter, he released him, perhaps recalling Queen Isabella's orders against slavery. After allowing his crew to rest, he decided to sail east. He was confident that he would, at any time, find the strait that would lead him directly to the Indian Ocean, and to the Orient. He was unable to find the strait, and had to settle for meeting the Guaymi, who were happy to trade pure gold ornaments to the Spanish for bells and beads.

In October, he noticed a large mountain range. Believing that nothing lay beyond them, Columbus somehow took the presence of the mountains as proof that the strait he had been searching for did not exist, and that the focus of his voyage needed to change. He abandoned the search for the passage to the East and began to search for gold and silver in earnest, his original intent to convert the natives again cast aside. He knew that to find more gold he would need to sail south.

When the expedition approached the territory called Veruga, a tense confrontation with a different group of Guaymi was successfully calmed without violence, although there was another small skirmish the following day. The Spanish were able to trade, although somewhat uneasily, with the Indians, and sailed away from the area. He initially headed in an eastward direction, but made little progress.

Since the bays in that area were not suitable for long-term docking, Columbus attempted to sail west. Upon realizing he was leaving gold country, he tried to return to Veruga, but was stranded in the bay of Puerto Bello. The Indians there traded cotton and food, but there was no gold. He managed to leave Puerto Bello, only to be caught in the rainy season. He and his ships made little progress, until at last they arrived, once again, at Limon Bay.

Columbus Spends a Year in Jamaica

In January of 1503, the rainy season in Panama was relentless. The expedition was able to move, very slowly, westward. Upon the discovery of a gold deposit further inland, Columbus thought it would be a good idea to establish a fort in the location. His plan was to leave Bartholomew in charge while he sailed to Spain for supplies. As the construction of the fort began, which was to be named Santa Maria de Belen, the rain stopped. Unfortunately for Columbus, the rivers and inlets dried up so severely that the ships could not be sailed out into the bay.

The relationship between the Spanish and the Guaymi was tense at best, and excursions by the Spanish onto the islands to rob and rape the Indians was leading to increased hostilities. To make matters worse, the Spanish had captured a Guaymi cacique and his family. The chief was able to escape, and raised an army of Indians to fight the Spanish. Just as the battle began, the rains returned, and all but one of the Spanish ships were able to sail out into the bay.

The Guaymi continued to attack until they were forced to retreat. The captured Indians who were aboard one of the ships were able to remove a hatch, and most were able to swim back to the shore. Those who were not able to escape committed suicide by hanging themselves from the rafters of the ship. Columbus, who was once again suffering from a fever, was on a ship further out to sea, in a state of delirium during the battles.

When his fever cleared, Columbus realized the fort on the island would lead to the massacre of the Spanish he had left there, including his brother, Bartholomew. He and his crew were able to send rafts to the shore to bring the men back to the two remaining ships, but the ship that was stranded closer to shore had to be abandoned. With two ships remaining, Columbus made the choice to sail for Hispaniola in hopes of securing supplies for the journey home to Spain.

The significance of the fact that he was banned from the colony of Santo Domingo, especially at such a time of great need, was not lost on Columbus. He wrote, in his journal, of his distress.

The tempest was terrible and separated me from my [other] vessels that night, putting every one of them in desperate straits, with nothing to look forward to but death. Each was certain the others had been destroyed. What man ever born, not excepting Job, who would not have died of despair, when in such weather seeking safety for my son, my brother, shipmates, and myself, we were forbidden [access to] the land and the harbors which I, by God's will and sweating blood, had won for Spain?

With his ships storm-battered and in need of repairs, Columbus made it as far as the coast of Jamaica before he realized the ships would not make it much farther. He docked them facing one another in an attempt to provide some sort of protection, and prepared to stay until a rescue ship could be sent. Because there was no gold to be found, the Spanish and the Tainos there were able to establish a somewhat peaceful coexistence. In order to keep the crew from taking liberties with the women and girls on the island, Columbus only allowed sailors to leave the ship with his permission, and only granted leave to a few sailors at a time.

The Indians there fed them from June until December of that year, and then, perhaps after realizing the Spanish had nothing more to trade, they stopped. One story widely reported indicates that Columbus used an upcoming lunar eclipse to trick the natives into believing that he was a god, and to continue feeding them for fear of angering him. Whether or not it worked, he left little to chance.

By canoe, Diego Mendez, who was a loyal crewman and friend of Columbus, took a suit of armor to the Indians and traded for a canoe. He also convinced some of the Indians to take him to Santo Domingo in their canoes. The first attempt to reach Santo Domingo, which was nearly 500 miles away, failed, and he lost the canoe. When he found another one, he made the attempt again, and after four days, reached Santo Domingo.

Regrettably, Columbus's old enemy, Governor Nicolas de Ovando, was the person to whom Mendez and his men had to make their request for assistance to be sent to Columbus. The governor said he would send help, but that it would take some time. It took months for him to provide anything, during which Mendez had no way of sending word to Columbus that he had reached the city.

While Mendez was gone, the tensions among the crew had caused it to split into two camps. One camp was led by two brothers, who had managed to convince many of the travelers that Columbus refused to sail to Santo Domingo because he was wanted for some kind of crime.

They began to attack and plunder the villages of the natives on the island. They stole ten canoes and managed to enslave enough of the Taino to paddle the canoes to Santo Domingo. Unfortunately, many of the Taino died during the journey, as did several of the rebels. They had to return to Jamaica, having failed in their attempt to reach Hispaniola. When the rebels returned, they continued to raid the villages.

Ovando finally sent a ship with food for the stranded expedition. The travelers thought they were being rescued when the saw the ship approaching. However, the ship was sent by Ovando to deliver salted meat, wine, and other gifts, and the captain of the ship refused to take any of the crew with him. He reported back to de Ovando that Columbus was still alive.

Ovando decided to wait to see what would become of the crew, believing that the death of Columbus would make it possible for him to claim the title of Viceroy of the Indies. While Columbus was happy Mendez had safely made it to Santo Domingo and the passengers were relieved to know the governor at least knew of their predicament, no one was permitted to board the ship and leave. In the meantime, conflict broke out between the split factions of the expedition, and many of them died. Columbus managed to stop the fighting and put the leaders of the rebellion in chains.

Columbus offered the two brothers a share of the provisions that had been sent by Ovando, but the rebels saw the offer as a sign that he was weakening. They mounted an attack against Columbus and his brothers, while Bartholomew leading the counterattack. Interestingly enough, the natives did not participate in any of the bloody battles that took place. They were somewhat fascinated at the idea that the Spaniards, who had shown them so much cruelty and had taken so many of their lives, had the capacity to be just as bloodthirsty with one another.

In 1504, almost a year after Mendez landed in Hispaniola, de Ovando received permission from the royals in Spain to send one rescue ship for Columbus. The people who had survived starvation, disease, and warfare sailed to Santo Domingo. Since the ship was in such poor shape and constantly needed to stop for repairs, the 500-mile journey took more than six weeks. The passengers, however, were so grateful to have left the rotting, grounded ships on the shore of Jamaica that they did not complain.

When he reached Santo Domingo, where he knew most of those in power were against him, Columbus hired a ship to take himself, his son, and his brothers back to Spain. Columbus traveled back to Spain as a passenger, and not as the great captain and explorer. The journey took fifty-six days, and it was a difficult crossing. By the time he reached Spain, almost twelve years after his first voyage to the New World, Christopher Columbus ended his time on the seas, and set about restoring his name and reputation.

Chapter 7:
Restoring a Bad
Reputation

"I went to sea from the most tender age and have continued in a sea life to this day. Whoever gives himself up to this art wants to know the secrets of Nature here below. It is more than forty years that I have been thus engaged. Wherever any one has sailed, there I have sailed."

—**Christopher Columbus**

Columbus's Later Life

Upon his arrival in Spain, Columbus's first act was to secure the money that had been promised to his crew. Three weeks after his return, Queen Isabella died, and his support came to an end. He attempted, in spite of his failing health, to secure the titles and honors he felt the crown owed or had promised him.

Columbus wrote two books after his return to Spain, with help from his son, Diego, and a monk by the name of Gaspar Gorricio. The first book was The Book of Privileges. Written in

1502, the book detailed the benefits of the Crown of Castile (a state on the Iberian Peninsula). His second book was The Book of Prophecies, released in 1505, which detailed the achievements of his career as an explorer, accompanied with Bible passages to illustrate his claims. With all that had happened, Columbus believed that his voyages had been inspired by God himself. On one occasion, he wrote:

It was the Lord who put into my mind that fact, that it would be possible to sail from here to the Indies. All who heard of my project rejected it with laughter, ridiculing me. There is no question that the inspiration was from the Holy Spirit, because He comforted me with rays of marvelous inspiration from the Holy Scriptures.

Because of the contract—specifically, the one called the Capitulations of Santa Fe—that he'd signed with Queen Isabella and King Ferdinand, Columbus had received ten percent of all profits he accrued from his travels. This left Columbus a wealthy man in his later years, able to live in relative comfort, although his health had begun to decline rapidly. He spent much of his time in his advancing age petitioning to have the titles and honors restored to him that had been stripped upon his arrest, but with the death of the Queen, he was all but forgotten as far as the Crown of Castile was concerned.

The Sons of Columbus

Diego Columbus, later known as Don Diego, sailed with his father for much of his young adulthood, and Columbus wished for Diego to be named governor of Hispaniola. His wishes went mostly ignored by King Ferdinand, but the monarch did allow Diego to assume the title of Admiral. It wasn't until three years after

Christopher Columbus's death that Diego was appointed governor of Hispaniola. It is believed that, rather than his father's requests, it was Diego's marriage to Dona Maria de Toeldo, the King's cousin, which made his appointment to the position of governor possible.

Hispaniola prospered greatly after Christopher had left it, and while Diego proved to be a far more competent leader than his father had been before him, much of the credit must be given to Nicolás de Ovando, who had organized the colony at Hispaniola and who had established order long before Diego took his place.

Diego spent much of his time in Spain, attempting to secure his title of Viceroy of all the Indies. He died in 1562, in Spain.

Ferdinand Columbus, later known as Don Hernando Colon, became a page to Queen Isabella at the age of ten. He accompanied his father on the fourth voyage to the New World when he was fourteen. On his return to Spain at sixteen, he resumed his education. In 1509, he returned to Santo Domingo to spend six months with his half-brother, Diego, who was, by then, an admiral. He went home to Spain to continue his life as a scholar and traveler. Unlike his father, Ferdinand was extremely gregarious and friendly, and was well-liked by all who knew him.

Because of appointments from the crown, as well as the inheritance he received from his father's estate, which included over four hundred slaves in Hispaniola, Ferdinand was able to travel extensively, become a collector of arts, books, and other highly prized objects of that time, and to buy a large house in Seville, where he settled and furnished one of the largest private libraries in the country. Upon his death in 1539, his estate donated more than 15,000 volumes to the cathedral at Seville.

Columbus Makes a Last Attempt to Restore His Good Name

Queen Isabella of Castile died on November 26, 1504, taking with her the last of the support Columbus received from the crown. By the time Columbus was informed of Isabella's death, he was too ill to travel to her funeral. He was also too ill to continue his journeys to the royal court to request the king restore his titles. While his son, Don Diego, was able to complete some of his father's business with the crown, he was unable to convince King Ferdinand to grant Columbus an audience.

While the King did see to it that Ferdinand was paid for his service to the Queen as a page, he decreed that any monies recovered from Hispaniola that were to be sent to Columbus must first be sent to the crown in order to pay any debts Columbus owed. The crown never did restore to Columbus the titles he'd lost upon his arrest during his third voyage.

Columbus and his son continued to appeal to the crown to restore his lost titles and benefits, but his pleas went ignored. As the court moved from city to city, Columbus, in his declining state of health, was forced to move with it, as that was the only way he could be sure to be in attendance should he be granted another audience with the king. The travel took a toll on Columbus. He was reduced, in the end, to writing letters to his old acquaintances, begging them for help in addressing the king. When Columbus thought all hope was lost, he was presented with information that led him to think he might, once again, find favor in the royal court.

The king had been acting as regent for Isabella's daughter, Juana, and her husband, Archduke Philip of Austria, until she was able to assume the throne. His plan, however, was to marry a young royal from France, the niece of King Louis XII, and to produce a male heir that would supersede Juana's claim to the throne. Upon learning of her father's intentions, Juana and her husband made plans to travel to Spain to secure her claim. Upon hearing this, Columbus, who remembered the young royal from her childhood days at her mother's feet when he made his triumphant return from the first voyage, believed he would find the help he needed with the young, would-be rulers.

Unfortunately, Columbus was too ill to travel to meet the Dona Juana himself, and was in preparations to send one of his long-time friends to the meeting, when his illness overcame him.

Chapter 8:
Death and Legacy

"I am a most noteworthy sinner, but I have cried out to the Lord for grace and mercy, and they have covered me completely. I have found the sweetest consolation since I made it my whole purpose to enjoy His marvelous Presence."

—Christopher Columbus

Illness and Death

For the last year of his life, Columbus spent much of him time in bed. Along with intermittent fever, he suffered excruciating pain in his joints. His health had begun to decline as young as his early forties. It is believed that his difficult first voyage to the New World was the beginning of his health problems. It is also believed that he suffered from arthritis.

Columbus suffered from fevers, eye infections that impaired his vision, bouts of delirium, and leg pain, with cramps and inflammation. Diego believed that his father suffered from gout, a form of arthritis that affects the extremities of its victims, and causes fever, as well as joint pain. However, gout is typically episodic, whereas Columbus, once besieged by illness, never seemed to be able to recover his health.

Modern-day medical professionals, after studying the journals of Columbus as well as accounts written by those who knew him, are of the opinion that he suffered from reactive arthritis, and died as a result of a heart attack caused by his condition. It is more likely, however, that Columbus succumbed to a rare tropical disease called Reiter's Syndrome, the symptoms of which had begun to manifest during his third voyage to the New World. Christopher Columbus died on May 20, 1506, in Valladolid, Spain. He was 54 years old.

The day before he died, Columbus ratified his last will and testament, proclaiming his eldest son, Don Diego, the heir to all his properties, titles, and privileges, with the exception of those that he left to Fernando, Fernando's mother, Beatriz de Harana, his immediate family, and various charities and monasteries in Genoa and Lisbon. During his last hours, an often delirious Columbus was surrounded by his youngest brother, Diego, his sons, his loyal ship mate, Mendez, friends, and a few of his beloved servants.

He was initially buried—with the chains by which he'd been bound on his way back to Spain after his third trip to the Americas—in Valladolid's tiny cemetery, but his remains were later moved to a cemetery in Seville. Upon his death in 1526, Columbus's older son, Diego, was buried there as well. When Diego's widow requested both son and father be interred at the cathedral in Santo Domingo, in Hispaniola, the crown granted her permission to have them moved, and Columbus, postmortem, sailed across the Atlantic again for the last time. For nearly 200 years, there he remained. When Hispaniola was captured by the French in 1795, the Spanish moved the remains to Cuba, which was still under Spanish control.

When Cuba successfully gained independence from Spain, the remains were moved, for the final time, back to Seville. Unfortunately, workers restoring the cathedral at Santo Domingo claimed to have found a box of human remains that belonged to Columbus in 1877, leading many to believe that the body that had been moved was actually that of Columbus's son, Diego, and that the body of Columbus had remained in Santo Domingo. As a result, there are two tombs that may contain the actual body of Christopher Columbus: one in Seville, and one in Santo Domingo, and it is impossible to determine which is which.

Legacy

While Christopher Columbus was not the first European to encounter the New World, he opened a permanent route from Europe to the "New World" that led to centuries of exploration and colonization of the Americas.

The legacy left by Columbus is one of a fearless explorer, a navigational genius who was able to brave the perils of unknown seas, foster communication and relationships with other cultures, secure land and riches for his benefactors in Spain, and convert "heathens" to Christianity. Many saw (and still see) Christopher Columbus as a hero, a conqueror who fulfilled his promises to the King and Queen of Spain, despite never making it to the Far East. His exploits paved the way for combining the traditions and cultures of Europe with the ways and customs of the native population of the New World.

Unfortunately, there is a dark side to the legacy of Columbus as well. His encounters with the indigenous peoples of the islands brought disease, cruelty, genocide, and abject misery to a population that had never known such despair and desolation. His practices set in place the blueprint for what became the transatlantic slave trade. Columbus's son, Diego, became the first slave trader to import slaves from Africa to the New World. Most of Columbus's income and wealth was the direct result of the enslavement of the Indians he captured.

The Columbus Day Controversy

In 1792, twenty years after the Declaration of Independence was signed, Americans celebrated the 300th anniversary of Columbus's arrival in the New World. In 1892, the 400th anniversary was celebrated as well. Columbus Day first became an official holiday in the state of Colorado in 1906. While the holiday was not declared a federal holiday until 1937, President Franklin D. Roosevelt designated October 12 "Columbus Day" after a campaign conducted by the Knights of Columbus, a Catholic service organization founded to benefit impoverished Catholics in the United States. In 1970, the holiday was changed to fall on the second Monday in October.

The cities of San Francisco and New York observe the largest celebrations of Columbus Day, with parades, along with the closures of most federal offices, banks, and some school districts. Other cities do not observe the holiday at all. While several states, including South Dakota, Oregon, Alaska, and Hawaii do not observe Columbus Day for its intended meaning; commemorating Columbus's landing in the New World, many states observe "Indigenous Peoples Day," which commemorates the Native populations devastated by the Spanish colonization of the Americas.

Indeed, the general consensus of those who oppose Columbus Day feel much as Eduardo Galeano, who believes that the Indians, upon Columbus's landing on their shores, made some discoveries of their own. As he puts it:

In 1492, the natives discovered they were Indians, discovered they lived in America, discovered they were naked, discovered that the Sin existed, discovered they owed allegiance to a King and Kingdom from another world and a God from another sky, and that this God had invented the guilty and the dress, and had sent to be burnt alive who worships the Sun the Moon the Earth and the Rain that wets it.

While many cities have removed the holiday from involuntary observance at the state level, there are those who wish to continue to celebrate the spirit of Columbus's journey, if not the man's actions. These proponents of the day argue that many of America's holidays, from Cesar Chavez Day (California), to Martin Luther King Jr. Day, celebrate the achievements of representatives of different nationalities. Many Italian-Americans feel that Christopher Columbus deserves no less than his own designated holiday, although he had never embraced the title of "Italian" and proclaimed himself a proud "Genoese" until his death.

While Columbus died still waiting to be restored to the position of power and the wealth he felt he was owed by the crown, and while he never succeeded in finding the western sea route to the East Indies, Columbus also died never knowing the extent of his contribution to the world. No, he hadn't exactly "discovered" the Americas, but what he did do was to introduce the continent of Europe to the New World. His findings were instrumental in making Spain one of the most powerful and wealthy countries in the world.

Facts vs. Fiction

It is a myth that Christopher Columbus set out on his voyage to prove the world was round. Greek scholars and mathematicians such as Pythagoras and Aristotle used astronomy to study the shape of the earth. Most people in Columbus's time were well aware that the earth was not flat, including the sailor himself.

He stated, "I have always read that the world, both land and water, was spherical, as the authority and researches of Ptolemy and all the others who have written on this subject demonstrate and prove, as do the eclipses of the moon and other experiments that are made from east to west, and the elevation of the North Star from north to south."

It is also a myth that Columbus was the first European to make a transatlantic voyage. While the honor is generally bestowed on the Viking Leif Erikson, who discovered what was later named Newfoundland nearly five hundred years before Columbus was even born, it is also worth mentioning that Polynesian explorers discovered the continental Americas long before Leif himself was born—though that was technically transpacific, not transatlantic.

Another interesting fact regarding the voyages of Christopher Columbus is that he presented his plan first not to the Spanish, but to the king of Portugal, who, believing Columbus's calculations were incorrect (rightfully so, as Magellan later proved), denied his request for financial backing. Believing they could improve upon Columbus's plan, King John sent his own expedition on a mission to find a westerly route to the Orient, only to find that the ships had to return to Portugal when fierce storms forced them to turn around. It was Portuguese sailors who later laid claim to land in South America. Columbus was also prepared to present his idea to the French, should the Spanish monarchy decline his request.

It is not a well-known fact that the Santa Maria did not survive the first voyage to the New World. On December 25, 1492, an exhausted and sleep deprived Columbus turned his watch over to a lesser-ranked officer of the ship, who then turned the watch over to one of his subordinates, who then turned over the watch to a cabin boy with very little experience at sea. The ship drifted onto a coral reef, and could not be salvaged. The wreckage from the ships was used to build the first Spanish colony in the New World, La Navidad.

Many are under the impression that Columbus sailed across the Atlantic once. In all, the explorer made four trips across the sea, never finding the western sea route to the Orient he'd sought for more than a dozen years. It also escapes many that he was arrested and returned to Spain in chains after his third voyage to the New World to stand trial for corruption and mismanagement of the colonies of La Navidad, La Isabela, and Santo Domingo. He was led from the island onto a ship in chains, and returned to Spain in much the same fashion as the Indians he had captured and sent abroad to be sold at the slave market at Seville.

Even after Columbus's death, he continued to sail the seas. After the death of his son, Diego, his daughter-in-law requested both Columbus and his son be buried in Santo Domingo. After the French took control of the island, the Spanish removed the remains from the cathedral and moved them to Cuba, where they remained until the Spanish-American war ended. The remains were then moved back to Seville—though, as stated earlier, it's impossible to determine whether they were his or his son's.

Columbus's Contemporaries

In spite of arguments to determine what Columbus actually "discovered" versus what he simply became aware of, there can be no denial that he was the first European navigator to discover the phenomenon of Trade Winds. He realized there was a wind that blew westward from the east. Conversely, there were prevailing winds in the north Atlantic that allowed the ships to be pushed to the coastlines of western Europe. He was able to utilize the clockwise pattern of the winds to cross the Atlantic many times.

This discovery aided in the further exploration of the West after Columbus's death. Where the Admiral's travels ended, a new generation of explorers and conquerors' journeys began. Here are a few of the explorers that owe their successes and discoveries to Christopher Columbus.

Vasco da Gama (1460-1524)

While Columbus remained obsessed with the idea of locating a western sea route to Asia, Vasco da Gama was commissioned by the Portuguese to find an easterly passage. Unlike Columbus, Vasco da Gama was successful in his quest, and became the first European to reach India by sea. While Columbus was aware of his success, it was the need to sail southward along the western coast of Africa and around the Cape of Good Hope that kept Columbus inspired to find a faster, less arduous route. Vasco da Gama died after contracting malaria in India, in December of 1524.

Amerigo Vespucci (1451-1512)

Vespucci was born in Florence, Italy, the third son of Ser Nastagio and Lisabetta Mini Vespucci, friends of the powerful Medici family. Amerigo was educated by his uncle, although his brothers attended university in Tuscany. In his early twenties, Amerigo served as an ambassador to France, and became enamored with the idea of exploration. As they had done with Christopher Columbus, Queen Isabella and King Ferdinand also funded the expeditions of Vespucci. Unlike Columbus, however, the Portuguese also agreed to fund his travels to the New World.

There is some controversy regarding the dates of his earliest solo expeditions to the west, which may mean that Vespucci discovered Venezuela a full year before Christopher Columbus reached the shores of South America. Regardless, it cannot be disputed that Amerigo Vespucci was the first European explorer to "discover" what is now Rio de Janeiro, along with Rio de la Plata. Unlike Columbus, he believed, correctly, that South America was its own continent, and was not a part of the East Indies, as Columbus had thought.

His 1501-1502 voyage provided important information that influenced geographic discovery. Word began to travel that the lands Vespucci discovered were a continent unto themselves, and not part of Asia. German cartographer Martin Waldseemuller created a map using information from both Columbus and Vespucci's travels. He named the new continent "America," a feminized form of Vespucci's first name.

Vespucci died in Seville, Spain, after becoming a citizen of that country, in 1512.

Ferdinand Magellan (1480-1521)

When Pope Alexander VI decreed that the world, as it was known at that time, was to be essentially divided between Spain and Portugal in the Treaty of Tordesillas, Spain began desperately searching for a western route to the Indonesian Archipelago, the chain of islands that comprise the nation. The existing path led through territories held by Portugal. The Spanish crown agreed to finance the expeditions of Magellan.

In 1519, some thirteen years after Columbus's death, Portuguese explorer Ferdinand Magellan left Spain determine to discover the western sea route that had eluded Christopher Columbus. In October of 1520, more than a year after he'd set sail, he discovered the strait that Columbus had missed by a mere fifty miles. The strait was named after him, and at long last, Magellan and his men reached the Pacific Islands.

Magellan was killed in battle before he was able to reach the Spice Islands, but the final ship that remained of his fleet of five, the Victoria, returned to Seville, Spain in 1522, proving that it was, indeed, possible to circumnavigate the globe.

Epilogue

"Hardly a name in profane history is more august than his. Hardly another character in the world's record has made so little of its opportunities. His discovery was a blunder; his blunder was a new world; the New World is his monument!"
—**Justin Winsor**, American writer, historian, and librarian.

Though there are many things for which Columbus is rightfully accused, his contribution to history is too significant to dismiss him entirely. Like many historical figures, there are a huge number of ugly things in the man's past, ones that have, in recent years, overshadowed his real accomplishments.

However, by bravely committing to sailing westward until he found the strait to the East, the Indian Ocean, and made his way to Asia, set in motion the next phase of the Age of Exploration. Because of Christopher Columbus, the East and the West met. Further, his discovery of the Trade Winds propelled exploration and cartography for decades to come, and paved the way for other explorers and adventurers to meet and surpass his legacy.

Even with the controversy surrounding his methods, the dubious nature of his leadership, and his obvious weaknesses for gold, power, and prestige, it cannot be denied that Columbus earned the right to have his name remembered for all time.

Sources

Heat-Moon, William Least (2002). Columbus in the Americas. Hoboken, New Jersey: John Wiley & Sons, Inc.

Morrison, Sam Elliot (1942, 1970). Admiral of the Ocean Sea: A Life of Christopher Columbus. Boston, MA: Little, Brown and Company

Biograpy.com Editors. "Christopher Columbus Biography" Biography.com Website 18 July 2016
Retrieved from
http://www.biography.com/people/christopher-columbus-9254209

Kasum, Eric "Columbus Day? True Legacy: Cruelty and Salvery"huffingtonpost.com 15 October, 2015 Retrieved from
http://www.huffingtonpost.com/eric-kasum/columbus-day-a-bad-idea_b_742708.html

Lane, Kris "5 Myths About Christopher Columbus" washingtonpost.com 8 October, 2015
Retrieved from https://www.washingtonpost.com/opinions/five-myths-about-christopher-columbus/2015/10/08/3e80f358-6d23-11e5-b31c-d80d62b53e28_story.html

Flint, Valerie I.J. "Christopher Columbus: Italian Explorer" Britannica.com 14 January, 2016
Retrieved from https://www.britannica.com/biography/Christopher-Columbus

History.com Staff "Christopher Columbus" history.com 2009/18 July, 2016
Retrieved from http://www.history.com/topics/exploration/christopher-columbus

"Cristoforo Colombo Quotes." 18 July, 2016
goodreads.com
Retrieved from
https://www.goodreads.com/author/quotes/47
901.Cristoforo_Colombo

"Christopher Columbus." BrainyQuote.com.
Xplore Inc, 2016. 18 July 2016
Retrieved from
http://www.brainyquote.com/quotes/authors/
c/christopher_columbus.html

DigitalHistory.com Staff. "Slavery and Spanish
Colonization" digital history.uh.edu 2016
Retrieved from
http://www.digitalhistory.uh.edu/disp_textbo
ok.cfm?smtID=2&psid=3569

The Film Archives. "Christopher Columbus:
Facts, Ships, Biography, Exploration,
Education, Legacy" Published 27 November,
2015

Beal, Alfonso. "Christopher Columbus (A&E)" Youtube.com Published 12 August, 2014

Andrews, Evan "10 Surprising Facts About Magellan's Circumnavigation of the Globe" History.com 2012/ 18 July, 2016 Retrieved from http://www.history.com/news/history-lists/10-surprising-facts-about-magellans-circumnavigation-of-the-globe

Made in the USA
San Bernardino, CA
28 August 2018